Contents

W9-CDH-727

Brass Instruments

trumpet

clarinet

People play many instruments to make music.

People blow brass instruments.

Not all brass instruments are made
of brass.

mouthpiece

People play brass instruments
by making their lips buzz into a
mouthpiece.

6

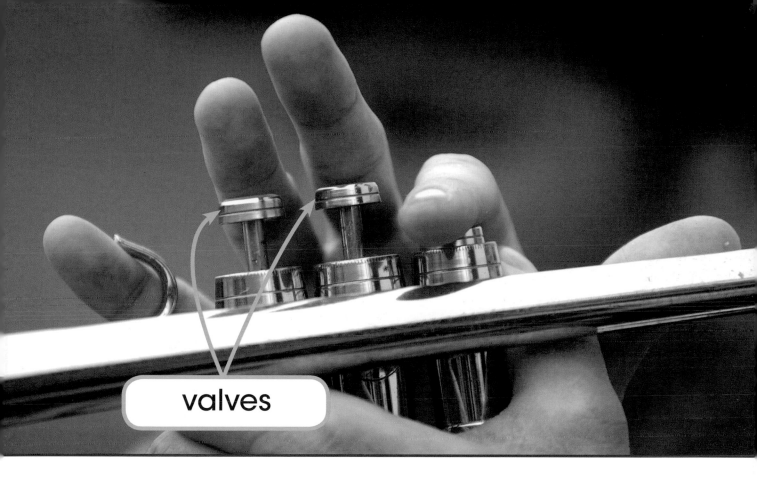

valves

People play notes by pressing keys called valves.

Different Brass Instruments

A piccolo trumpet is small.

It plays high notes.

A tuba is very big.

It plays low notes.

A sousaphone wraps around the person playing it.

sliding tube

A trombone has a sliding tube.

Unusual Brass Instruments

This alphorn is very long.

This tuba is very big.

A conch shell trumpet is made from
a seashell.

A didgeridoo is made from the
branch of a tree.

Playing Brass Instruments

Some people play brass instruments outside.

Some people play brass instruments inside.

Some people play brass instruments for work.

Some people play brass instruments just for fun!

Making Brass Instruments

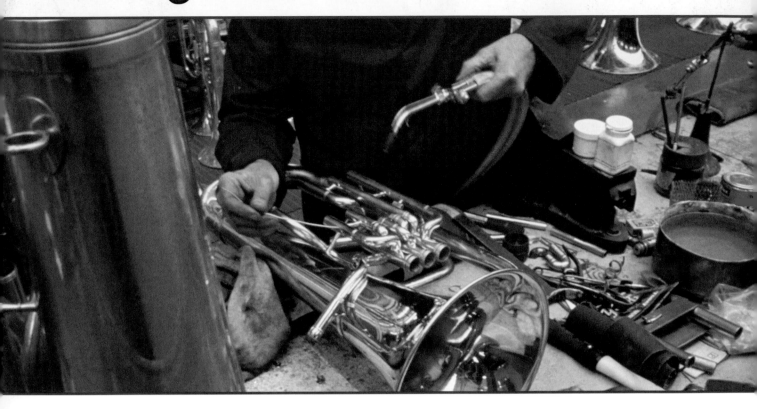

Some brass instruments are hard to make.

Some brass instruments are easy
to make.

Play Your Own Brass Instrument

You can play your own brass instruments, too!

Picture Glossary

 **mouthpiece** part of an instrument that you blow into

 **note** sound made by a musical instrument

 **valve** key on a brass instrument that you press to change the note

Index

Notes for Parents and Teachers

Before reading

Show the children examples of brass instruments. Online examples with audio can be found at: http://www.sfskids.org/templates/instorchframe.asp?pageid=3. Can they name any of the instruments? How do they think the instruments are played? Explain that an instrument is in the brass group when it is played by the player making their lips buzz, or vibrate. Demonstrate if possible.

After reading

Encourage the children to make their own brass instrument. Get them to blow raspberry sounds into a small plastic tube, such as a piece of plastic pipe. The sound can be made higher or lower by tightening or loosening the lips.

Extra information

The instruments shown on page 5 are: French horn (top left), trumpet (top right), didgeridoo (center), tuba (bottom right), and trombone (bottom left).

A didgeridoo and a conch shell might not look like brass instruments, but they are because they have a mouthpiece, which you vibrate your lips into. Small brass instruments are high sounding. Big brass instruments are low sounding because the air has farther to travel.

[8]